Philosopher Guide or the "Desert of the Real"
The World Famous Philosophers

Heinz Duthel

ISBN 9783741211324

Famous Philosophers

Cicero
David Hume
Rene Descartes
Thales of Miletus
Thomas Aquinas
Socrates
Saint Bonaventure
Baruch Spinoza
Friedrich Nitzsche
Aristotle
Confucius
Avicenna
Francis Bacon
Claude Levi-Strauss
Plato
John Rawls
Immanuel Kant
Boethius
Seneca the Younger
John Stuart Mill

Some of the most prominent philosophers of the 20th and 21st centuries are Bertrand Russell, Ludwig Wittgenstein, Jean-Paul Sartre, Claude Levi-Strauss, Albert Camus, Richard Rorty, Noam Chomsky and Slavoj Žižek.

Philosophy is said to be the mother of all disciplines. It is the oldest of all disciplines and gave rise to modern science as we know it today as both social and natural sciences have their roots in philosophy. Modern sciences either directly emerged from philosophy or are very closely related to philosophical questions. Understanding philosophy and of course, the way problems are addressed by philosophers is therefore the key to understanding of science as we know it today.

Ancient Greek and Roman Philosophers
The "love for wisdom" (English translation of the Greek word philosophia) dates back to the ancient times in both the East and West. Although the fundamental questions of philosophy have been dealt with very early, the history of the Western philosophy begins with the ancient Greek philosophers in Asia Minor in the 6th century BC. Thales of Miletus who is regarded as the first ancient Greek philosopher had profoundly influenced other Greek thinkers, encouraging them to search for the answers in nature rather than supernatural world. The next centuries saw the rise of philosophical schools throughout Greece and emergence of some of the greatest thinkers of Western philosophy including Heraclitus,

Socrates, Plato and of course, Aristotle.

Ancient Greek philosophy continued to flourish in the Western world throughout the Roman period in the form of Hellenistic and then Greco-Roman philosophy that was dominated by Greco-Roman philosophers of Cicero, Seneca, Plutarch and Plotinus, to mention only a few. The late Roman period, however, also saw the rise of Early Christian philosophers such as Augustine of Hippo (also known as St. Augustine) who profoundly influenced medieval philosophy that was completely dominated by theological questions.

Medieval Philosophers

The fall of the Western Roman Empire marked the end of the Greco-Roman philosophy and many of the greatest philosophical works have been lost. But in contrary to the common misconception, medieval philosophers were not only dealing with questions such as how many angels can stand on the head of a pin nor completely ignored the works of Greco-Roman philosophers. At the same time, the works that have been lost in the West after the fall of Rome found their way back to Europe through Muslim conquests and later the Crusades.

Medieval philosophers, although preoccupied with theological questions, did not reject the Greco-Roman philosophy but worked on how to reconcile it with the Christian reasoning, especially the Aristotle's logic. This was finally achieved by St. Thomas Aquinas who is considered one of the most important medieval philosophers.

Modern Philosophers

The Late Middle Ages and Early Modern period were marked by an increased interest in ancient philosophy independently from the Christian Church and scholasticism that dominated the medieval thought. Renaissance movement that would eventually spread throughout Europe emphasised rationalism and empiricism which in turn gave rise to the Age of Reason and modern philosophy. Erasmus, Niccolo Machiavelli, Galileo Galilei and Francis Bacon marked the beginning of departure from the medieval approach to fundamental philosophical questions which was furthered by the 17th century philosophers such as Thomas Hobbes, Blaise Pascal, Rene Descartes, Baruch Spinoza, John Locke and George Berkeley, to mention only a few of the greatest names of the 17th century philosophy.

The works of the 17th century philosophers have profoundly influenced the next generation of thinkers such as Voltaire, Diderot, Rousseau, Montesquieu, Immanuel Kant, David Hume, Thomas Pain and Adam Smith who laid the foundation to the so-called Enlightenment, while many also played an important role in the far-reaching political changes that took place in the 18th century including the American Revolution and the French Revolution.

The 19th century philosophers, although greatly influenced by the Enlightenment ideas, introduced a number of new concepts including idealism (the German schools), utilitarianism (Britain), Marxism, existentialism, pragmatism and positivism. Some of the greatest names of the 19th century philosophy include Georg Wilhelm Friedrich Hegel, John Stuart Mill, Jeremy Bentham, Karl Marx, Friedrich Engels, Friedrich Nietzsche and Auguste Comte who is also regarded as the founder of the modern discipline of sociology.

Contemporary Philosophers

Contemporary philosophy refers to period from the beginning of the 20th century until the present-day. The 20th century saw the professionalisation of the discipline but it also saw the rise of new schools which, however, would split philosophers between "analytic" and "continental" although some contemporary philosophers regard themselves as the bridge between the two traditions.

Eastern Philosophy

Eastern philosophy which encompasses Chinese, Japanese, Indian and other Far Eastern philosophies as well as Jewish and Islamic philosophies (although the latter two are sometimes also considered as a part of Western philosophy) developed independently from Western philosophy. Generally, Eastern philosophers were not as occupied with questions relating to the nature of God although both Jewish and Islamic philosophers were just as focused on reconciling new ideas with Judaism and Islam as their western colleagues. Far Eastern philosophers mostly dealt with the questions of ethics, morality, justice, etc. rather than religious truths. But some such as Confucius and Tao for instance, gave rise to religions and state ideologies.

Cicero

Marcus Tullius Cicero (106-43 BCE) is widely considered Rome's greatest orator and verse writer but he was also an influential statesman, successful lawyer and philosopher. He has greatly influenced the Western thought and philosophy despite the fact that his own contribution to the discipline is generally considered of lesser importance. However, thanks to Cicero, Western philosophers gained access to many important ancient philosophical works that would otherwise be lost forever.

Personal Life

Cicero was born in 106 BCE to a wealthy landowner who had good connections with the social elites in Rome but he was prevented from entering the public life due to a physical disability. Cicero is said to have been a talented student which enabled him to study law under Quintus Mucius Scaevola, one of the greatest authorities on Roman law. Around 83 BCE, he started practising law and won his first major case during Sulla's dictatorship. He got his client acquitted of murder by accusing Sulla's favourites for his client's crime which was very risky because the dictator could easy had at the time unknown Cicero assassinated.

In 79 BCE, Cicero went to Greece to study and probably also to avoid Sulla's counter-measures for his accusations in the court. He returned to Rome in 76 BCE, got married. One year later, he became quaestor which got him a chair in the Senate. Victory in the case of Gaius Verres against the best advocate at the time in 70 BCE increased his prestige and by 63 BCE, he held the office of consul which was the highest political position he could legally hold in his age. However, his political career soon brought him into trouble. He exposed the Catilina conspiracy which foresaw his assassination and overthrow of the Roman Republic. He was awarded the Pater Patriae honour but feared a trial or exile for having the conspirators put to death without trial.
In 60 BCE, Cicero was invited by Julius Caesar to join him, Pompey and Crassus as the fourth triumvir. He refused Caesar's offer and publicly spoke against Caesar. This earned him

an exile in Macedonia but he was recalled to Rome after 16 months. After returning to Rome, he tried to return to politics but he failed to turn Pompey against his co-triumvirs. He dedicated himself to writing and occasionally defended the triumvirate. He did not interfere in the war between Pompey and Caesar, and did not try to return to politics after Pompey's death. Instead, he throw himself into writing rhetoric and philosophy.

Although Cicero disliked Caesar's dictatorship and approved conspiracy against him, he was not involved in his assassination. After Caesar's death, he tried to reconcile his assassins and Mark Antony but he soon concluded that the latter is threat to the Republic. He began to speak publicly against Mark Antony on behalf of Octavian (later Augustus). However, before the two started a war for the rule over Rome, they reached an agreement and together with Lepidus set up a three-man dictatorship. Both Octavian and Mark Antony started eliminating their enemies as the enemies of the state and in 43 BCE, Cicero was assassinated on Mark Antony's order.

Cicero's Philosophical Works

Although Cicero is considered one of the most important Western philosophers, he did not make any major contributions to the discipline as such. All his works are written in outstanding Latin prose, proving his brilliance with words but do not offer much originality. However, it is important to note that Cicero was primarily a politician and considered politics a priority. Ironically, he turned out to be the least successful in politics which was directly responsible for his premature death. Cicero's philosophical works are mostly reproductions of the prominent Greek philosophers, mostly stoic. However, his works "De amicitia" (On Friendship), "De senectute" (On Old Age), "De officiis" (On Duty), "De natural deorum" (On the Nature of the Gods), to mention only a few are a priceless source of ancient Greek philosophy, while rediscovery of Cicero's letters by Petrarch in the 14th century is by some thought to gave rise to Renaissance. Cicero's writings also had a major influence on the Enlightenment philosophers, particularly Montesquieu, John Locke and David Hume.

Other Works

Cicero is best known for his speeches (of which 57 have survived) and political philosophy. He is also known to have been a highly respected poet, however, none of his poetry survived. The works that did survived including hundreds of letters he wrote to various correspondents came to be regarded as a synonym for Latin as well as a priceless source for history of the late Roman Republic and early Roman Empire.

David Hume

David Hume (1711-1776) went into history as one of the most important figures of Western philosophy but he also made important contributions to history and literature. In contrary to rationalists such as Descartes, Hume argued that it is not reason that governs human behaviour but desire instead. He said that "reason is, and ought only to be the slave of the passions". But despite the fact that had profoundly influenced the next generation of philosophers, his theories were not received particularly well by his contemporaries.

Personal Life

David Hume was born in 1711 to Joseph Home of Chirnside and his wife Katherine Falconer in Edinburgh, Scotland. He later changed his surname from Home into Hume because it was pronounced incorrectly outside Scotland. Hume started to attend the University of Edinburgh at a very early age. In contrary to most of his schoolmates who were 14 years old, he was aged 12 or 10. He was pressed by his family to study law but instead, as he said he had secretly devoted himself to studying Voet, Vinnius, Cicero and Virgil. Due to the intensity of his intellectual discovery, however, he suffered a nervous breakdown in 1729 from which he did not recover fully for several years.

In 1734, he went to France, spending most of the time at the La Fleche where he started to write his best known and most influential work titled A Treatise of Human Nature. The critics in Britain, however, disliked it and described it as unintelligible. Hume was disappointed by the reception of his first work but he soon got over it. He returned to England in 1737. In 1740, he moved to Edinburgh where he wrote "Essays Moral and Political". It was published in 1744 and it was much better received than the Treatise. Possibly encouraged by the success, he applied for the chair of moral philosophy at the University of Edinburgh, however, he was rejected due to opposition of the Edinburgh ministers for his "heresy" and "atheism".

Again disappointed, Hume left Edinburgh and spend an entire decade wandering from one place to another. But all this time, he continued to study and write. It was during the period of wandering when Hume started to write the six volume and over million word "The History of England" that was published between 1754 and 1762, and became a best-seller. While he was working for Lieutenant-General St Clair, he also wrote the "Philosophical Essays Concerning Human Understanding" (published as An Enquiry Concerning Human Understanding in 1758) which was followed by "The Enquiry Concerning the Principles of Morals in 1751. He continued to write almost until his death, ending his list of works with the autobiography "My Own Life". He died from cancer in 1776. Hume never married and had no children.

Works and Influence

Hume's approach to the fundamental questions of philosophy, his reformulation of scepticism and approach to science of human nature dramatically influenced the future course of Western philosophy. The Scottish philosopher played an important role in the development of critical philosophy by Immanuel Kant and Auguste Comte's positivism but he also greatly influenced Jeremy Bentham and the school of utilitarianism. Ironically, the greatest impact on history of philosophy achieved his first work, A Treatise of Human Nature that met a disappointing response from his contemporaries.

In addition to philosophy, Hume is also regarded as one of the most important figures in the field of history, literature and economy. The History of England broke with the tradition that traced only political and military history, and was intentionally created to be more readable. All Hume's works reveal an exceptional sense for style for which he became famous already during his lifetime and remains highly valued ever since. His writing on economy, especially in the Political Discourses and Treatise are thought to influence his friend, Adam Smith who became a pioneer of political economy. The extent of Hume's influence on Smith is unknown but he introduced several ideas that profoundly influenced the 18th century economy as a whole.

Rene Descartes

Rene Descartes (1596-1650) was not only one of the most prominent philosophers of the 17th century but in history of Western philosophy. Often referred to as the "father of modern philosophy", Descartes profoundly influenced the European thought with his writings. Probably best known for his statement "Cogito ergo sum" (I think, therefore I am), the philosopher started the school of rationalism which broke with the scholastic Aristotelianism in two ways. Firstly, Descartes rejected the mind-body dualism, arguing that matter (the body) and intelligence (the mind) are two independent substances (metaphysical dualism) and secondly, he rejected the final causal model of explaining natural phenomena and replaced it with science-based observation and experiment. He spent a major part of his life in conflict with scholastic approach which still dominated the thought in the early 17th century and trying to convince the Churchly authorities that the new sciences are not challenging the traditional theological teachings.
Personal Life

Rene Descartes was born in La Heye in the French region of Touraine in 1596 to Joachim Descartes and his wife Jeanne Brochard. His mother died when he was only one year old. His father remarried, while he and his older brother and sister were raised by his grandmother and a nurse. At the age of 10 years, he enrolled into the Jesuit college of La Fleche which was attended by children of nobility and which was according to Descartes one of the best schools in early 17th century Europe. At the age of 18, he completed the Le Fleche college and spent the following years refining noble skills- fencing, dancing and horsemanship. In 1614, he went to Poitiers and took a law degree two years later. He then spend more than one year in the Netherlands studying mathematics and military architecture.

During the first decade of the Thirty Years' War (1618-1628), Descartes was travelling extensively over Europe and as he said, studied "the book of the world". He was attached to various military units but appears to have taken little action. Instead, he dedicated himself to mathematics. In 1619, he invented analytic geometry but he also came to conclusion that mathematics-based deductive reasoning is applicable to other sciences. During this period, he is also said to be greatly influenced by three dreams which according to Descartes revealed him that all sciences are one. He did not reject different objects of study but he claimed that a generalised method would allow one mind to know everything.

In 1629, Descartes moved to Holland where he spent the next 20 years of his life. He completely dedicated himself to studying and writing, living from his inheritance, his books and patrons who financially supported his work. He never married but he had a relationship with a servant who bore him a daughter, Francine who died at the age of 5 from Scarlet fever. In 1649, he accepted the invitation of Queen Christina to come to Stockholm where he died only one year later.

Major Works

Rene Descartes left a large number of writings of major importance for both philosophy and mathematics. Of all his works, the "Meditations on First Philosophy" published in 1641 and 1642 is probably of the greatest importance and remains one of the seminal texts in virtually all university philosophy departments. In contrary to his earlier works which dealt with methodology, the Meditations show that it can be applied to the fundamental philosophical questions including scepticism, existence of soul, nature of God, truth, human knowledge of the external world and the relation between the body and mind. The Meditations caused a lot of controversy and as a result, Descartes spent most of his remaining life defending his positions which were very dangerous at the time. He was a devoted Catholic, however, we must not forget that he was a contemporary of Galileo Galilei (1564-1642) who was tried by the Inquisition and forced to recant his heliocentric model. Fortunately for Descartes, his writings were not seen as "heretical" for the ecclesiastic authorities but it is also true that he was afraid of persecution and censure which clearly reveals the withdrawal of the work "The World" in which he supports the Copernican theory that earned Galileo a condemnation by the Church and house arrest.

Other major works by Rene Descartes include Compendium Musicae (1618),

The Word (originally Le Monde, published posthumously in 1664), L'Homme (published posthumously in 1662), Discourse on the Method (1637), Geometry (1637), Principles of Philosophy (1641) and the Passions of the Soul (1649).

Thales of Miletus

Thales of Miletus (c. 624 BCE – c. 546 BCE) was an ancient (pre-Soctratic) Greek philosopher who is often considered the first philosopher and the father of Western philosophy. His approach to philosophical questions of course cannot compare to modern or even later Greek philosophers, however, he is the first known person to use natural explanations for natural phenomena rather than turning to supernatural world and his example was followed by other Greek thinkers who would give rise to philosophy both as a discipline and science. In addition to being viewed as the beginner of Western philosophy, Thales of Miletus is also the first to define general principles and develop hypotheses. He is therefore sometimes also referred to as the "father of science" although this epithet is usually used in reference to Democritus, another prominent ancient Greek philosopher who formulated the atomic theory that states that all matter is composed of particles called atoms.
Personal Life

Not much is known about the philosopher's early life, not even his exact dates of birth and death. He is believed to be born in the city of Miletus, an ancient Greek Ionian city on the western coast of Asia Minor in today's Turkey. The time of his life was calculated on the basis of events related to him in the later sources, most notably in the work "Lives and Opinions of Eminent Philosophers" by Diogenes Laertius (c. 3rd century BCE) who wrote biographies of ancient Greek philosophers and one of the most important sources for ancient Greek philosophy. Laertius tells us that according to the chronicle by Apollodorus of Athens, Thales of Miletus died in the 58th Olympiad aged 78. Since the 58th Olympiad was the period between 548 and 545 BCE, Thales of Miletus was born sometime between 626 and 623 BCE.

According to Laertius who quotes Herodotus, Douris and Democritus, Thales' parents were Examyes and Cleobuline who are thought to had been of Phoenician origin and well financially situated. As much as his later life is concerned, there are a lot of conflicting information. According to some sources, Thales was married and had a son named Cybisthus but according to other, he never married and adopted his nephew Cybisthus.

Thales' Philosophical Works

Thales of Miletus is said to had written "On the Solstice" and "On the Equinox", however, none of the two works survived and some doubt that he left any written works. Even in antiquity, there were some doubts about Thales' written works although some authors also connect him with "The Nautical Star Guide". The latter, however, is highly unlikely to had been written by Thales of Miletus considering that Laertius tells us that the very same work is attributed to a lesser known Phokos of Samos. But despite the scarcity of reliable evidence about Thales of Miletus, there is little doubt about his – at the time – revolutionary approach to philosophical questions. In his "Metaphysics", Aristotle tells us that Thales believed that everything comes out of water and that the earth floats on water. And according to Seneca, the philosopher used the floating earth theory to explain earthquakes. This means that Thales of Miletus rejected the supernatural and mystical theories that were used to explain various phenomena by his predecessors which justifies his fame as the first philosopher. He is the first known thinker to abandon the supernatural agenda but he is also the first known thinker to try to explain the world by a unifying hypothesis.

Thales' as Astronomer and Mathematician

Although Thales of Miletus is best known as the first Western philosopher, he actually became famous for predicting a solar eclipse. According to Herodotus, the philosopher correctly predicted the year of the solar eclipse which impressed his contemporaries and later ancient Greek thinkers because in his time, no one knew how to predict solar eclipses in Greece. The modern methods confirmed that a solar eclipse indeed took place during Thales' lifetime, however, the story about Thales predicting the eclipse is surrounded with controversy because if he did correctly predict the eclipse, it apparently worked only once because whichever method he used, it was not used again. Although some sources claim he could have used the Babylonian lunar cycle known as the Sages and that he could have gained the knowledge about predicting solar eclipses from the Egyptians (he is known to have visited Egypt), most modern scholars think both explanations are highly unlikely. They attribute the story of Thales predicting the solar eclipse to a lucky guess, while some think that it never happened at all and that it was assigned to him because he was a highly respected philosopher who happened to live in the time of the eclipse and therefore, he must have known that it is coming.

In addition to being hailed as the first philosopher, Thales of Miletus is sometimes also hailed as the first mathematician. According to ancient sources, it was Thales who brought the discipline to Greece from Egypt and made many important mathematical discoveries himself, most notably that the circle is bisected by its diameter and that a triangle inscribed in a semi-circle is always a right triangle (Thales' theorem). However, just like Thales' astronomical discoveries, his mathematical achievements are doubted by some modern scholars.

Thomas Aquinas

Saint Thomas Aquinas (1225-1274) is one of the most famous medieval philosophers who is hailed as the Church's best theologian and philosopher. Just like his contemporaries, Aquinas was primarily focused on theological questions but the thing that set him apart from others the most is his outstanding combination of two seemingly conflicting concepts – the Roman Catholic faith and Aristotle's reasoning. Although he is today primarily associated with the Catholic doctrine, he has also profoundly influenced modern philosophy in many areas, particularly in metaphysics, ethics and natural law.

Personal Life

Aquinas was born in 1225 in Roccasecca in the castle of the Aquino family (therefore he is sometimes also referred to as Thomas of Aquino) to Landolfo Aquino and his wife Teodora of Chiety. Due to the war between Pope Gregory IX and the Holy Roman Emperor, Frederick II, Landolfo and Teodora decided to sent their youngest of nine children to Monte Cassino to receive elementary education. Young Thomas stayed at the abbey from 1231 until 1239 when Monte Cassino was occupied by the Imperial troops. He continued education at the University of Naples where he is thought to have been introduced to the works of both Aristotle and Averroes which profoundly influenced his later theological and philosophical works.

In 1244, Aquinas joined the Dominican order at Naples but he was soon sent to further education to the University of Paris. There, he did not only gained access to all the major Greek, Latin and Arab works but he also studied with Albertus Magnus, a Dominican friar who is celebrated for his advocacy of coexistence of religion and science. Although he failed in his first theological disputation, he became Magnus' favourite pupil and followed his teacher to Cologne in 1248. There, he taught as an apprentice professor until 1252 when he returned to Paris for further education. After completing training as a theologian in 1256, he was appointed master professor at the University of Paris but only after Pope's intervention at the secular masters who disliked their Churchly colleagues.

The years between 1259 and 1268, Aquinas spent in Italy. In 1268, he returned to the University of Paris where he faced opposition by both the fraction that advocated the conservative Augustinian teachings and the Averroists who advocated Aristotlelianism. Aquinas did not belong to neither of the two groups and tried to reconcile the two concepts in his writings. Although he feared "radical" Aristotlelianism just like the Augustinians, his writings provoked hostility of the Augustinians led by Bonaventure who achieved condemnation of some Aristotle's articles and indirectly, of Aquinas as well.

Aquinas ended his second professorship in Paris in 1272 when he returned to Italy. He lectured at Naples and continued writing but only for about a year when he gave up writing completely. Aquinas died at the Fossanova Abbey in Italy en route to the Second Council of Lyon in 1274. In 1323, he was canonized by the Catholic Church.
Aquinas' Works
Today, Aquinas' works have a much greater value for theology than for

philosophy but we must not forget that his time was dominated by religion. His approach to the questions of religion and reasoning were revolutionary for both the Augustinians for whom faith was the only truth and Averroists who wanted to separate the truth from the faith. Aquinas was opponent of both approaches and advocated coexistence of faith and reason on the basis that both were given by God although he emphasised the importance of reason which he regarded as independent from faith. He managed to join the main concepts of the two opposing schools although his view was adopted only after his death. Aquinas was without a doubt above all a great theologian who criticised philosophers for being pagan. Nevertheless, he played an important role in history of Western philosophy by embracing Aristotle's "heretic" reasoning.

Aquinas left many writings on various issues. The most significant works include the Summa theologica (Summa of Theology), Summa contra Gentiles, and commentaries on Aristotle and Bible.

Socrates

Socrates (ca. 469-399 BCE) is hailed as one of the founders of Western philosophy, however, very little is known about him as a historical figure and philosopher. The best account of life and work of one of the most influential philosophers of all times is given by the later classical writers, in the first place by his students Plato and Xenophon and the playwright Aristophanes who was his contemporary. Despite that, the mentioned writers reveal that the ancient Greek philosopher made important contributions to philosophy as well as epistemology and logic. He is the inventor of the so-called Socratic method or elenchus which remains one of the most commonly used approaches not only to answer the fundamental questions of philosophy but it also serves as a tool for scientific research. Ironically, the most famous Socrates' saying is "I only know that I know nothing".

Socratic Problem

As mentioned earlier, Socrates' life and work are surrounded by mystery. He did not write any philosophical works or left any writings. The knowledge we have about him both as a historical figure and philosopher is based exclusively on later classical writings. Uncertainty regarding Socrates' life and work which is known as the Socratic problem is related to the fact that the information we have about him (besides the above mentioned authors, Socrates also appears in the works by Aristotle and the famous historian Thucydides) are philosophical and dramatic rather than historical texts. This makes it very difficult to create a picture of his life, work and philosophical thought.

Socrates' student Plato is traditionally considered the best source about the philosopher's life and work although many scholars emphasise that it is very difficult to distinguish between Plato's and Socrates' philosophical views and even more difficult to create an accurate account of Socrates' life. As a result, some consider Xenophon to be more reliable source of information about Socrates as a historical figure.

Personal Life

Plato and Xenophon are the main sources for Socrates' personal life.

From their writing, we find out that the renowned ancient Greek philosopher was born to Sophroniscus, a stonemason (or perhaps a sculptor) and his wife Phaenarete who was a midwife. He spent his life in Athens where he was born but details of his early life are scarce. He is said to participate in the Peloponnesian War (431-04 BCE) and that he married relatively late with Xanthippe who was much younger from him. She bore him three sons - Lamprocles, Sophroniscus and Menexenus.

It is not certain what Socrates did for a living. According to Xenophon, he was completely devoted to philosophy, while Aristophanes says that he earned a living by teaching at a school he ran with Chaerephon. Plato, however, rejects the accounts of Socrates being paid for teaching. Then there are also accounts of him working as a stonemason, like his father. In the antiquity, he was credited with the creation of the Three Graces statues near Acropolis but this has been rejected by modern scholars.

The Gadfly of Athens

Plato portrays Socrates as the gadfly of Athens. He explains that Socrates loved to "test" the wisdom of those he considered to be wiser than him. But since most of the people he "tested" were statesmen and other influential people of Athens, he soon came to be known as the gadfly of Athens because his methods of testing wisdom made many influential people look everything but wise in the public. He also came into conflict with the elites and the general public in Athens by praising the city's rival of Sparta although he claimed loyalty to Athens. It is speculated that his role of gadfly might had been one of the leading causes for his trial and execution. However, he remained the "gadfly of Athens" until the very end. At the trial, he apparently proposed that he should be paid a wage by the government and free dinners for lifetime when he had been asked to propose a punishment for his wrongdoing.

Trial and Execution

Those who persecuted and tried Socrates did not left any records. Again, Plato and Xenophon are the main sources for the events leading to the philosopher's trial and execution. They tell us that Meletus, Lycon and Anytus charged Socrates with impiety and corrupting the minds of the youth of Athens. In his defence speech, he is said to defend his role as the "gadfly", making it easy on his persecutors to sentence him to death. Both Plato and Xenophon tell us that he had an opportunity to escape and that his friend Crito even bribed the guards in the prison but he decided to stay. He was given to drink poison hemlock.

Socratic Method

Socrates main contribution to Western philosophy is his method of inquiry that was called after him Socratic method, sometimes also known as elenchus. According to the latter, a statement can be considered true only if it cannot be proved wrong. The Socratic method which is dialectic breaks down a problem into a series of questions which are then sought to be answered. This method which is also used in scientific research by making a hypothesis and then either proving it correct or false, is by some suggested to be first used by Zeno of Elea (ca. 490-430 BCE) but it was Socrates who refined it and used it to solve ethical questions.

The philosopher's beliefs are difficult to distinguish from Plato's. According to some, they may have been reinterpreted by Plato but according to the others, the latter perhaps completely adopted Socrates' philosophical thoughts and that his beliefs actually reflect those from Socrates. Thus the famous philosopher's saying "I only know that I know nothing" can be in a way also claimed for his life and work.

Saint Bonaventure

Saint Bonaventure (1221-1274) was one of the most influential medieval theologians and philosophers. He is celebrated for his outstanding ability to reconcile the opposing theological and philosophical traditions. In 1482, he was canonised by Pope Sixtus IV and one century later, Pope Sixtus V declared him Doctor of the Church.

Early Life

Little is known about Bonaventure's early life. He was born as Giovanni di Fidanza in 1221 at Bagnoregio in Latium (at the time an integral part of the Papal States) to Giovanni di Fidanza and Maria Ritella. During his childhood, he fell severely ill and according to Bonaventure, he recovered due to the intercession of St. Francis of Assisi. At the age of 14, he went to Paris to study at the University of Paris. In 1243, he was awarded master of arts degree and in the same year, he joined the Franciscan Order and took the name Bonaventure.

Later Life

After graduating at the University of Paris, he studied theology in the French capital. In 1254, he became master of theology and taught at the Franciscan school until 1257. In the same year, he was awarded a doctor degree at the University of Paris and soon thereafter, he was elected as minister general of the Franciscan Order. His election on the position of the minister general of the Franciscans was influenced greatly by his successful defence of the mendicant orders against the secular professors. These were led by William of Saint-Amour who wanted to exclude the members of the mendicant orders from the teaching positions at the University of Paris.

At the time when Bonaventure became the minister general of the Franciscans, the order was divided into the so-called Spirituals who were strictly advocating poverty and the Relaxati who proposed a more relaxed lifestyle. With his authority, he managed to restore the unity of the Order and reformed it in the spirit of its founder, St. Francis. In 1260, Bonaventure reformed the Order's constitution as well as successfully defended it from

Gerard of Abbeville, a theologian and opponent of the mendicants at the University of Paris. Later, he also stood up against the attempts to exclude revelation from philosophy by some masters at the University.

In 1273, Pope Gregory X named Bonaventure as Cardinal Bishop of Albano (Italy) despite the fact that ten years earlier, he refused the post of the Archbishop of York. In 1274, he was consecrated by the Pope in Lyon and resigned as minister general of the Franciscan Order. He took part at the Council of Lyon later that year and played an important role in the church reforms, reconciliation of the secular clergy and mendicants as well as in restoration of the union between the Greek and Roman Catholic churches.

Mysterious Death

Bonaventure died during the Council of Lyon in 1274. The cause of death is unknown but according to the chronicle of his secretary Peregrinus of Bologna, Bonaventure was poisoned. He was buried in the Church of the Friars Minor at Lyons on the day of his death.

Philosophy and Works

Bonaventure's greatest works are commentaries on the Bible and the Sentences (a textbook that was written by Peter Lombard in the 12th century), followed by Breviloquium ("Summary") and De Reductione Artium Ad Theologiam ("On the Reduction of the Arts to to Theology") which reveal both his theological and philosophical views. These as well as later works such as Itinerarium Mentis in Deum ("Journey of the Mind to God") reveal that he followed the teachings of St. Augustine but they also reveal the influence of ancient philosophers, most notably Aristotle. Just like his personal life, his works reflect an outstanding ability to reconcile contradictory traditions in both theology and philosophy which is why he was considered one of the foremost scholars already by his contemporaries.

Bonaventure was both a theologian and philosopher but like all the philosophers of his time, he was first a theologian and only then a philosopher. He considered philosophy inferior to theology although he viewed philosophy in itself as the highest science. Bonaventure did not reject Aristotle although he criticised his "defects". He did, however, oppose the new ideas that appeared in Scholasticism in the mid-13th century and remained loyal to the traditional view that was based on the teachings of St. Augustine.

The "Commentaries on the Sentences" are traditionally viewed as Bonaventure's greatest masterpiece. The book that contains over four thousand pages is divided into four books and deals with all the main questions of Scholasticism. Besides theological and philosophical works, Bonaventure also wrote many works that are related to religious subjects, especially to the Franciscans. In addition to re-codifying the constitution of the Order, he had also rewritten St. Francis biography titled the Life of St. Francis of Assisi.

Some Bonaventure's works are unfortunately lost, while many were wrongfully attributed to him. Works that were attributed to Bonaventure but are thought or proven to be written by other authors are referred to as Pseudo-Bonaventure. Examples include Centiloquium, Philomena,

Stimulus Amoris, The Legend of St. Clare, Biblia pauperum, Meditationes vitae Christi, Theologia Mystica, Speculum Disciplinae and some others.

Baruch Spinoza

Baruch Spinoza, Latinised Benedict de Spinoza (1632-1677) was a Jewish-Dutch philosopher whose work played the key role in formation of the modern Western thought. By rejecting the Descartes' mind-body realism and the traditional presentation of God by the Jewish and Christian traditions, Spinoza paved the way to modern rationalism. The importance of his work, however, was realised only after his premature death.

Background

Baruch Spinoza was born in 1632 as the second son of Miguel de Espinoza and his second wife Ana Debora in Amsterdam, the Netherlands. His father was a successful merchant of Portuguese Jewish origin. Young Spinoza was raised up in the Portuguese Jewish community in Amsterdam that grew significantly after the Spanish Alhambra Decree (1942) and the Portuguese Inquisition (1536), both of which resulted in forced conversions to Christianity and expulsions from Spain and Portugal. Many Sephardic Jews including the so-called 'conversos' emigrated to the Netherlands, especially after the Decree of Toleration that was issued in 1579. Here, they reconverted to Judaism and built the first synagogue in 1598.

Early Life

Young Spinoza was without a doubt influenced greatly by the Jewish community in Amsterdam. He was brought up as a Jew and attended the yeshiva (Jewish educational institution with a focus on the study of religious texts). He learned from the traditional Rabbi Saul Levi Morteira as well as the less traditional Manasseh ben Israel who is best known for founding the first Hebrew printing press in the Durch capital. For some reason, young Spinoza never reached the advanced study of the Torah. At the age of 17, he left the formal education and started to work in the family business. This was probably influenced greatly by the death of his older brother Isaac in the same year.

At the age of 20, Spinoza began to study Latin. He was taught by Franciscus Van den Enden, a former Jesuit who was notorious for his secular thought. It is believed that van den Enden made a major impression on Spinoza and that he probably introduced him to the concepts of scholasticism and early modern philosophers such as Descartes. After his father's death one year later (1654), Spinoza took over family business with his younger brother Abraham. At the same time, he adopted his Latinised name Benedictus de Spinoza and started to teach at Van den Enden's school. It is speculated that he was in love with Van den Enden daughter Clara who, however, rejected him.

In his early 20s, Spinoza came in contact with anti-clerical Christian groups that opposed the traditional dogmas and the church's authority. His radical Christian friends questioning the religious authorities and his teacher Van den Enden who introduced him to modern philosophy probably played an important role in his conflict with the Jewish religious authorities in Amsterdam. Spiroza allegedly said that God has a body and that there is nothing in the holy texts to say otherwise. In 1656, the Talmud Torah congregation issued cherem against Spinoza by which he was expelled from the Jewish community. He did not, however, convert to Christianity although he was close with the Christian sect of the Collegiants and was buried in a Christian cemetery. According to Yitzhak Melamed, Associate Professor of Philosophy at the Johns Hopkins University, Spinoza was the first modern European secular Jew.

Later Life

At the time cherem was issued against Spinoza, his family business came into serious financial difficulties. He left over the business along with the debts to his younger brother and dedicated himself to philosophy and optics for the remaining 21 years of his life.

Shortly after the cherem was issued, the Amsterdam authorities responded to the concerns of the rabbis and expelled Spinoza from the city. He moved to the village of Ouderkerk aan de Amstel nearby but he soon returned to Amsterdam and stayed there until 1660 or 1661, earning a living by grinding lenses and giving private philosophy lessons. During this period, he also wrote his first philosophical work titled "Short Treatise on God, Man, and His Well-

Being". In 1660 or 1661, he moved to Rijnsburg where he wrote "Principle of Cartesian Philosophy" (published in 1663). There, he also began to work on his greatest masterpiece – "The Ethics" which was published only after his death.

In 1663, Spinoza moved to Voorburg where he continued to work on "The Ethics" as well as other works. In 1670, he published "Theological Political Treatise" in which he supported Jan de Witt, the Grand Pensionary of Holland against William II, Prince of Orange as Stadtholder of Holland who later became William III of England. According to Leibnitz, Spinoza seriously jeopardised his life by supporting de Witt. Despite the fact that he published the "Theological Political Treatise" anonymously, the authorship was soon revealed. The Synod of the Reformed Church condemned the work in 1673 and officially banned it one year later.

In 1770, Spinoza left Voorburg and moved to The Hague where he spent the last years of his life living from a small pension and annuity from his dead friend's brother. He continued to work on the "Ethics" but he also wrote a Hebrew grammar (unfinished), scientific essays "On the Rainbow" and "On the Calculation of Chances" and started a Dutch translation of the Bible which he later gave up and destroyed.

Spinoza fell ill in 1776 and died one year later, aged 45. The cause of his death is not exactly clear. He is said to die from a lung disease which could have been related to inhalation of glass dust while he was grounding lenses. He never married and did not have any children.

Works

A Short Treatise on God, Man and His Well-Being (1660-1661)
On the Improvement of the Understanding (1662)
The Principles of Cartesian Philosophy (1663)
Theological Political Treatise (1670)
The Ethics (1677)
Hebrew Grammar (1677)

Friedrich Nitzsche

Friedrich Nitzsche (1844-1900) was a German philosopher whose work is surrounded by a major controversy. His critical texts on morality, religion, science and culture are a collection of often contradictory ideas and hypotheses rather than a systematic theory. Nevertheless, Nitzsche was without a doubt one of the most influential Western philosophers who had a major influence on the future generations of scholars both within and outside philosophy.

Nitzsche's influence is particularly obvious in the concepts of existentialism, post-modernism and post-structuralism. His concept of Übermensch ("superman") is also thought to have a major influence outside philosophy, most notably in German Nazism. Scholars, however, reject the connection between Nitzsche's thought and Nazism as "perverse" because the philosopher openly criticised anti-Semitism and pan-Germanism. He even laid off his editor for his anti-Semitic position and got into an open conflict with his former friend Richard Wagner due to the latter's pan-Germanic ideas and anti-Semitism.

Early Life

Nitzsche was born in 1844 in the town of Röcken in what was then Prussia (the later Germany). He was the oldest child of Lutheran pastor Carl Ludwig Nitzsche and his wife Franziska Oehler. They also had a daughter, Elizabeth Förster-Nitzsche who was born in 1846 and another son, Ludwig Joseph who was born in 1848. Nitzsche's father died when he was 5 years old and one year later, he also lost his young brother. His mother took him and his sister to her mother-in-law and two unmarried sisters-in-law in the town of Naumburg. They lived with them until Nitzsche's grandmother's death in 1856 when they moved to their own house (today Nitzsche museum and learning centre).

In 1858, young Nitzsche was accepted to Pforta in Naumburg which was one of the best boarding schools in mid-19th century Germany. There, he was introduced to classic literature and philosophy as well as gained several lifelong friends. After graduation, he enrolled in the University of Bonn to study theology and classical philology. But after the first semester, he discontinued to attend his theological classes and wrote to his deeply religious sister that he had lost his faith. Nitzsche focused on studying philology under Professor Friedrich Wilhelm Ritschl whom he followed to the University of Leipzig in 1865.

Professorship in Basel

In 1869, Nitzsche was offered position of a professor of classical philology at the University of Basel, Switzerland despite the fact that he did yet have a doctorate or teaching certificate. He accepted and gave up Prussian citizenship before moving to Switzerland. He later claimed that his ancestors are of Polish origin and that he his proud of his Polish blood. The scholars, however, are sceptical about his claims to be of Polish descent. They emphasised that Nitzsche is a relatively common German surname and that all Nitzsche's ancestor had German names. Why he claimed his family is of Polish origin remains unknown but according to some scholars, it was perhaps a part of his criticism of pan-Germanism.

Although Nitzsche opposed pan-Germanism and to a lesser extent, the concept of nationality, he joined the Prussian army during the Franco-Prussian War in 1870-71 as a medical orderly. This aggravated his illness – bouts of sickness that are thought to be related to syphilis which he allegedly contracted in a brothel while studying in Leipzig. But despite worsening of his health, he entered the most productive period of his life during which he created his most famous and influential works.

Later Life and Death

In 1879, Nitzsche's health deteriorated to such extent that he was forced to give up his position at the Basel University. He spent the next decade travelling in the search for a climate that would help him alleviate symptoms of his disease. He occasionally also came to Naumburg to visit his mother and sister Elizabeth. The latter was married to a German nationalist and antisemite Bernhard Förster and as a result, Nitzsche's relationship with his sister was marked by frequent conflicts and make-ups.

In 1889, Nitzsche suffered a mental breakdown while he was in Turin, Italy. His friends took him to Basel to a psychiatric clinic but his mental condition was rapidly worsening. On the initiative of his mother, he was transferred to a hospital in Jena. One year later, she took him to her home in Naumburg and took care of him until her death in 1897. After his mother's death, Nitzsche was cared for by his sister Elizabeth who also took care of publication of his yet unpublished works. And it was her editions that played the key role in the later association of Nitzsche's works with Nazi ideology. The later discovery of unedited writings undoubtedly rejects the existence of any connection between Nitzsche's ideas and their interpretation by the Nazis.

After suffering at least two strokes in the late 1890s, Nitzsche was unable to walk and speak. In 1900, he contracted pneumonia and died after suffering another stroke. According to most scholar, Nitzsche's health problems including mental illness and early death were caused by tertiary syphilis but other conditions have been proposed as well such as manic depression, dementia and CADASIL syndrome.

Nitzsche never married and did not have any children. He had a brief relationship with Lou Andreas Salome, a Russian born psychoanalyst and author. She said he proposed a marriage and that she refused him but her report about the course of events is according to some questionable.

Nitzsche's Philosophy and Works

Nitzsche's philosophy bases on three concepts - "God is dead" or the will to power, master-slave morality and Übermensch ("superman") which has nothing to do with the Nazi interpretation of the term. Instead, Nitzsche connects Übermensch with the ability to create own values. He also introduces the term nihilism or the claim that life has no meaning.

Some of the most famous and influential Nitzsche's works include:

- The Birth of Tragedy
- On Truth and Lies in a Nonmoral Sense
- Human, All Too Human
- Thus Spoke Zarathustra
- Beyond Good and Evil
- Ecce Homo
- The Will to Power

Slavoj Žižek

Slavoj Žižek (1949-) is a contemporary Slovenian philosopher who is best known for his political theory and cultural criticism although he also made an important contribution to theoretical psychoanalysis and film theory. Žižek is currently senior researcher at the Institute for Sociology and Philosophy at the University of Ljubljana in Slovenia but he is also a professor at the European Graduate School, International Director of the Birkbeck Institute for Humanities at the University of London and President of the Society for Theoretical Psychoanalysis in Ljubljana. A member of the Slovenian Academy of Sciences of Art from 2005 is a visiting professor at a number of world's most prestigious universities including the Princeton University, Columbia University, London Consortium and many others.

Žižek attracted international attention in the late 1980s when he published his first book in English. He is by many considered one of the top global thinkers. He has, however, also raised a lot of controversy which is why some consider him as a "Borat of philosophy" and a dangerous agitator for Marxism. Žižek's philosophy is most often viewed as Lacanian Hegelian but the influence of the Marxist concept cannot be overlooked.

Personal Life

Žižek was born in 1949 in Ljubljana, the capital city of Slovenia which was at the time a part of Yugoslavia. He spent a great part of his childhood in the coastal town of Portorož. His parents moved back to the Slovenian capital while he was a teenager and enrolled him to a prestigious high school in Ljubljana. Žižek continued his education at the University of Ljubljana where he studied philosophy and sociology. After receiving a Doctor's degree, he went to Paris where he studied psychoanalysis.

At the time Žižek began to study philosophy, the communist Yugoslavia was entering a period of liberalisation. But he was studying French structuralists even before he became a student of philosophy and sociology at the University of Ljubljana. As a high school student,

Žižek published the first Slovene translation of Jacques Derrida.

Despite the fact that Žižek studied philosophy during the era of liberalisation, he was influenced greatly by his teacher, Slovenian Marxist philosopher Božidar Debenjak. The latter was a professor at the Faculty of Arts in Ljubljana where he taught German idealism and Karl Marx's Capital from the Hegelian (philosophy of Georg Wilhelm Friedrich Hegel) perspective.

In the early 1970s, Žižek became an assistant researcher at the University of Ljubljana and was promised tenure. However, soon thereafter the Communist regime removed liberal leaders throughout Yugoslavia including what was then the Socialist Republic of Slovenia. As a result of toughening of the regime and Žižek's Master's work being evaluated as anti-Marxist, he lost his position at the University of Ljubljana.

In 1977, after being unemployed for four years, Žižek found a job at the Slovenian Marxist Center where he worked as a recording clerk. At that time he also came into contact with a group of scholars who introduced him to the theories of Jacques Lacan, a French psychoanalyst and psychiatrist who had a major influence on his later work. In the late 1970s, Žižek returned to the University of Ljubljana and was employed by the Institute of Sociology.

In the late 1980s, Žižek attracted a lot of attention both at home and abroad. At home, he gained a lot of publicity as a columnist of the alternative magazine called Mladina ("Youth") which was critical towards the Communist regime. Žižek who was a member of the Communist Party (like the majority of scholars and intellectuals at that time) returned his membership out of protest due to the so-called JBTZ trial. It was a trial held against two Mladina journalists, the magazine's editor and a sergeant at the Yugoslav People's Army for betrayal of military secrets in 1988. Žižek became active in political and civil movements for democratisation and even ran for Presidency of the Republic of Slovenia at the first free elections in 1990.

In the international scene, Žižek attracted attention in the late 1980s with his book The Sublime Object of Ideology and established himself as one of the most influential social theorist and contemporary philosopher.

Work

Despite the fact that Žižek was actively involved in the democratisation process in Slovenia, he is committed to the communist idea and describes himself as a "radical leftist" and "communist in a qualified sense". His political ideas and criticism of the existing political and economic systems caused a great deal of controversy in the intellectual circles on the one hand, and earned him the title of one of the foremost thinkers of modern times and a near celebrity-status on the other.

His works are influenced greatly by German idealism, most notably Georg Wilhelm Friedrich Hegel and Immanuel Kant as well as the previously mentioned French psychoanalyst Jacques Lacan. But his theories also reveal a great deal of influence by Marxism. Some of his most notable works include:

The Sublime Object of Ideology (1988)
Looking Awry (1991)
Tarrying With the Negative (1993)
The Abyss of Freedom (1997)
The Fragile Absolute: Or, Why is the Christian Legacy Worth Fighting For? (2000)
Did Somebody Say Totalitarianism (2001)
Welcome to the Desert of the Real (2002)
The Puppet and the Dwarf: The Perverse Core of Christianity (2003)
Interrogating the Real (2005)
In Defense of Lost Causes (2008)
Violence: Big Ideas/Small Books (2008)
Philosophy in the Present; with Alain Badiou (2010)
The Idea of Communism (2010)
God in Pain: Inversions of Apocalypse; with Boris Gunjevic (2012)
The Year of Dreaming Dangerously (2012)

Aristotle

Aristotle (384 BC - 322 BC) is considered one of the most influential individuals in history. He made important contributions to just about all fields of knowledge that existed in his time and became the founder of many new ones. The ancient Greek philosopher covered a wide range of subjects including biology, zoology, music, theatre, physics, politics, rhetoric, linguistics and much, much more. Along Socrates and Plato, Aristotle is one of the key figures in the emergence of Western philosophy and thought, while his writings in physical sciences profoundly influenced the intellectual life in medieval Europe.
The celebrated philosopher has written the first known system of logic that still forms the basis of modern logic. Aristotle's metaphysics, on the other hand, became an integral part of Christian theology, especially scholasticism and continues to play an essential role in Christian reasoning to the present day. His philosophy has also profoundly influenced the Jewish and Muslim thought. The medieval Muslim

thinkers referred to him as 'the first teacher'.

Personal Life

Aristotle was born in 384 BC in the ancient Greek city of Stagira on the Chalkidiki peninsula east of the modern city of Thessaloniki. His parents were members of aristocracy (his father Nicomachus was the physician of the Macedon king Amyntas) and were able to provide their son the best education. At the age of 18, Aristotle was sent to Athens to study at Plato's Academy. After completing education, he stayed at the Academy until 348 or 347 BC. He is said to quit because he was dissatisfied with the new Academy's leadership after Plato's death although some historians argue that he left before Plato's death due to the rise anti-Macedonian sentiment in the city.

After leaving Athens, Aristotle went to the court of Hermias of Atarneus in north-east Asia Minor. From there, he travelled to the island of Lesbos and focused on study of botany and zoology. He married Hermias' adoptive daughter Pythias with whom he had a daughter who was named after his wife Pythias. In 343 BC, he accepted the invitation of Philip II of Macedon to come to his court and tutor his son Alexander (the Great).

In Macedonia, Aristotle become the head of the Macedon academy. Besides tutoring Alexander, he also taught Ptolemy (the founder of the Ptolemaic Kingdom in Egypt) and Cassander (the future King of Macedon). Aristotle returned to Athens in 335 BC while his former pupil was preparing for the conquest of the Persian Empire. While in Athens, Aristotle founded his own school called the Lyceum and gave lessons at the school for more than a decade. After the death of his wife Pythias, he started an affair with Herpyllis of Stagira. She bore him a son who was named Nicomachus after Aristotle's father. According to the 10th century Byzantine encyclopedia Suda, Aristotle also had an erotic relationship with a young men called Palaephatus of Abydos.

It is believed that Aristotle's most productive period was after his return to Athens in 335 BC. He is thought to write many of his works while in Athens for the second time including many dialogues and treatises such as Physics,

Metaphysics, Politics, On the Soul (De Anima) and Nicomachean Ethics. He also wrote on theology, rhetoric, psychology and economics, and made important contributions to a wide range physical science including zoology, geography, geology, astronomy and anatomy, to mention only a few.

In the second half of the 320s, Alexander the Great feared a plot against him and sent threatening letters to Aristotle. The philosopher indeed openly opposed Alexander's divine pretences, while his grandnephew Callisthenes was executed by Alexander for treason. Throughout antiquity, Aristotle was believed to had been involved in the death of Alexander the Great but there is no evidence to support this claim. After Alexander's death, Aristotle once again witnessed the rise of anti-Macedonian sentiment in Athens. He was charged of impiety by Eurymedon the hierophant and left Athens for the second time in 322 BC, probably fearing for his life. He retreated to Chalcis on the island of Euboea where he died of natural causes within the same year.

Works

Although Aristotle's philosophy is the object of academic study worldwide, it is thought that most of his works have been lost over the centuries. Those that survived through the medieval manuscripts are thought to represent only one third of works created by the celebrated ancient Greek philosopher. The surviving works are collected in the so-called Corpus Aristotelicum. Some, however, are believed not to be composed by Aristotle himself but rather under his supervision and direction, while some are thought to be a product of his successors at the Lyceum. The Corpus is broken down into five sections – Logic, Physics, Metaphysics, Ethics and politics, and Rhetoric and poetics.

Aristotle's works are sometimes also divided into exoteric and esoteric. The first group of works refers to those that were intended for the public, while esoteric works were used mostly within his school such as the treatises. The Corpus Aristotelicum are exclusively treatises. Esoteric works, on the other hand, are lost although a few dialogues survived in fragments.

Confucius

Confucius (551/552-479 BC) was a Chinese teacher, philosopher and politician during the so-called Hundred Schools of Thought era. He was the founder of Confucianism, ethical and philosophical system that still has many followers in China. The philosopher is thought to write or edit many Chinese classic texts but modern scholars have expressed doubt that he is really the author/editor of all the works that are traditionally attributed to him. But there is no doubt that Confucius' philosophical system dominated the Chinese thought for many centuries.

Name and Sources for the Philosopher's Life and Work

Confucius' name is a Latinised version of Kong Fuzi that was coined by Jesuit missionaries in China sometime in the 16th century. In Chinese, the philosopher is usually referred to as Kongzi. But he is also known by the names such as "the Master", "First Teacher", "Model Teacher for Ten Thousand Ages" and "the Laudably Declarable Lord Ni".

Confucius' life and work are surrounded by many myths and legends which make objective appraisal of historical Confucius very difficult. Only in the recent years the scholars managed to discard some records as mythical and create a clearer picture of the philosopher's life and work.

The most extensive account of the philosopher's life is provided by the Records of the Historian, written by Sima Qian in the late 2nd and early 1st century BC. Unfortunately, Sima Qian's account is thought to be romanticised. Nevertheless, Sima Qian's as well as other sources that are generally dismissed as fictionalised provide a solid basis for the philosopher's biography when used with the Analects – the collection of Confucius' conversations with his followers.
Early Life

According to Sima Qian, Confucius was a descendant of the Shang dynasty that preceded the Chou. The year of his birth is traditionally dated to 551 or 552 BC with the latter being thought to be more likely. His father, King He was a military officer who died when Confucius was only three years old. He was raised by his mother Yan Zhengzai and is said to live in poverty. According to the traditional belief, Confucius was forced to do all kinds of works from being a shepherd to book-keeping. Modern scholars believe that his family probably was not wealthy but they doubt that young Confucius was affected by poverty. They emphasise that he belonged to the class of shi which was ranked lower from aristocracy but higher from the commoners. And during his time, most shih were scholars, court officials and teachers. As a result, Confucius is thought to be work in occupations that were consistent with his class status.

Political Career

Confucius' life and thought were influenced greatly by the decline of central authority in China in the 6th century BC. The Chou dynasty officially ruled the entire China but in reality, the Chou kingdom was a confederation of city-states that competed among each other for influence and power.

Confucius lived in the state of Lu that was officially ruled by a duke under whom were three aristocratic families – Meng, Ji and Shu. And it were the three families who de facto held power in the state of Lu. In 501 BC, the three families joined forces and expelled Duke Yang Hu but soon thereafter, Gongshan Furao who served the Ji family took the capital of Lu. He invited Confucius to enter his government but after some consideration, the philosopher refused. But in the same year, the philosopher entered politics under a legitimate government. After serving as a magistrate, he was promoted to the position of the minister of justice. The scholars speculate that he owed his political promotion to the Ji family which was the strongest of the three families. But the scholar also believe that he was working on reducing the families' power. This clearly reveals his initiative to dismantle the walls of the three families' seats of power. He managed to extract a promise from all three families but the Meng family changed its mind and the initiative failed.

Exile and Final Years in Lu

In 497, probably due to the failure to achieve his political objectives, Confucius decided to go in a self-exile. He left the state of Lu and travelled through the kingdoms of central and north-east China including the states of Song, Cai, Chen and Wei. He returned to Lu in 483 BC as an old man. The philosopher was warmly received but the last years of his life were not happy. He lost his only son and his favourite disciple Yen Hui. Probably devastated by the deaths of his son and disciple as well as the inability to persuade the rulers of the state of Lu to accept his political ideas, Confucius died in 479, aged 71 or 72.

Works and Philosophy

It remains uncertain how many and if any works that are attributed to Confucius were written by him. The account of his life and work is mostly based on the Analects, a collection of the philosopher's conversations with his students and a few rulers. The Analects were compiled by Confucius' followers shortly after his death and offer a valuable insight into his thought.

Confucius' philosophical system reveals the influence of the Chinese tradition such ancestor worship, loyalty to the family, respect of the elders, etc.. It was Confucius who introduced the concepts of benevolence (jen), ritual (li) and proprietary (yi). He is also remembered for the so-called Golden Rule that is based on the principle "Do not do to others what you do not want done to yourself".

The philosopher's political thought was centred around a strong central government and the Mandate of Heaven which, however, also included his moral concepts. According to Confucius, the principle of succession should not be based on blood line but on moral merits instead. He argued that the society can progress only if it is led by virtue and as a result, the rulers should be an example of virtue to their people.

Avicenna (Ibn Sina)

Avicenna (Ibn Sina) was a Persian physician and philosopher who profoundly influenced medieval Islamic philosophy, while his synthesis of ancient Greek and theology also had a major influence on the Western thought, especially that of the medieval Christian philosophers. Avicenna worked during the so-called Islamic Golden Age that was marked by advanced knowledge which surpassed that in the West. The territorial expansion of the Arab Abbasid Caliphate during that time gave the Muslim scholars access to vast knowledge including that of ancient Greco-Roman, Byzantine, Indian, Egyptian and Persian civilisations which became accessible to the Western scholars only in the later Middle Ages and Early Modern Period.

Early Life

The main source of Avicenna's life is his autobiography that was written by his follower Abd al- Wahid Juzjani. He tells us that the Persian philosopher was born about 980 in the village of Afshana near the present-day Bukhara in Uzbekistan. His mother Setareh was from the very same village, while his father Abdullah who was a high official under the Samanid dynasty was from the ancient city of Balkh in present-day Afghanistan. Avicenna's real name was Abu Ali al-Husayn Ibn Abd Allan Ibn Sina but he is commonly referred to under his Latinised name. In the Muslim world, he is known as Ibn Sina.

Young Avicenna was educated at Bukhara and by the age of 16, he established himself as a respected physician. But besides studying medicine, he also dedicated much of his time to the study of physics, natural sciences and metaphysics. In 997, Avicenna was hired as a physician by Nun ibn Mansur, Bukhara's ruler who gave him access to his royal library that was considered one of the best kinds in the medieval world. Over the next months, he read everything there was to read and soon began writing himself. The oldest surviving works date from 1001 when Avicenna was only 21 years old.

His father's death and political turmoil in 1002 forced Avicenna to leave Bukhara. He went to Urganj (present-day Konye-Urgench) in today's Uzbekistan but he soon moved to Gorgan in today's Iran where he started working on the Canon of Medicine which is his most famous work. But the philosopher did not stay there for long either. He moved to Rai near the present-day Tehran and after 10 years of wondering arrived to Hamadan where he finally settled down. There, he established himself as a respected philosopher and physician as well as composed his greatest works.

Later Life and Death

After the death of the emir of Hamadan, Avicenna wrote to the ruler of Isfahan and offered him his service. When the new emir found out about his letter to the Isfahan's ruler, he had him imprisoned. He was eventually released from prison but he decided to flee. Disguised as Sufi ascetics, Avicenna, his brother, a student and two slaves left the city and arrived to Isfahan in 1025.

In Isfahan, the Persian philosopher was warmly welcomed by the city's ruler. He spent his last 12 years in a relative peace, serving the city's ruler as his advisor and physician as well as working extensively on various branches of knowledge. He died from severe colic in 1037, aged only 58.

Philosophy and Works

Avicenna's philosophy dealt with some of the most fundamental questions including the origin of the cosmos, the role of God in the human existence and the universe, and divine interaction with humans and other "created" beings. He wrote extensively on logic, metaphysics and ethics, while his greatest contribution to the development of both later Muslim and Western thought was his attempt to reconcile the ancient Greek philosophy and God as the creator of all existence. Over the following centuries, Avicenna came to be regarded as the leading authority of the Islamic philosophy, while his synthesis of Greek philosophy and theology was later to some extent also adopted by the medieval Christian philosophers including Thomas Aquinas.

Avicenna is thought to create over 400 works on a variety of topics but only about 250 have survived. Of the surviving works, over 100 address philosophical questions, while about 40 deal with medicine. Some of his best known works include:

Book of Salvation

The Canon of Medicine
Book of Healing
Divine Wisdom
Book of Sum and Substance
Philosophy for the Prosodist
Book of Virtue and Sin

Although Avicenna's native language was Persian, most of his works were written in Arabic which was the language of the science in the Middle East in his time.

Francis Bacon

Francis Bacon (1561-1626) was an English philosopher, jurist and scientist who devoted most of his life to politics. His political career ended disgracefully despite the fact that he was very influential both under Queen Elizabeth I and her successor James I. But he remained an influential man until his death through his works, mainly those that dealt with philosophy and scientific method. It was Bacon who introduced scientific investigation of natural events and laid the foundation of modern scientific methodology. He is therefore also often called the "Father of Empiricism". He died from pneumonia which he contracted while he studied preservation of meet by freezing and went in history as a scientist who was killed by his own experiment.

Early Life

Bacon was born at York House in London on 22 January 1561 as the second son of Sir Nicholas Bacon and his second wife Anne (Cooke). Most historians believe that he was educated at home during his early childhood due to his poor health. At the age of 12, he was enrolled in the Trinity College, Cambridge where he lived three years with his older brother Anthony. The curriculum was in Latin and mainly followed the medieval system.

Three years later, in 1576 Bacon entered the Honourable Society of Gray's Inn (commonly known simply as Gray's Inn), one of four professional associations for barristers and judges in the British capital. But soon thereafter he went abroad. He accompanied Sir Amias Paulet who was at the time the ambassador in Paris. Over the course of three years, Bacon visited many cities including Blois, Tours and Poitiers as well as travelled to Italy and Spain. While travelling, he was studying statecraft, civil law and language but he also took care of basic diplomatic tasks.

Bacon returned to England upon learning of his father's death in 1579. Before his death, his father made arrangements to buy his younger son an estate but he died before carrying out his plans. Bacon borrowed some money and got into debts which would accompany him most of his life and contribute to his political downfall.

Entry into the Parliament

In 1580, Bacon tried to get a post at the court through his uncle Lord Burghley but he failed. He worked at Gray's Inn until 1582 when he became an outer barrister. Meanwhile, he entered the politics. In 1581, he was elected Member of Parliament for Bossiney, Devon, in 1584 for Melcombe, Dorset and then for Taunton. With his uncle's help, he became Bencher in 1586 and one year later, he was elected a reader. Three years later he also got the office of reversion to the Clerkship of the Star Chamber which he formally took only in 1608.

As MP, Bacon soon became friends with Elizabeth's favourite Robert Devereux, 2nd Earl of Essex and by 1591, he was Essex's adviser. With his influential friend's help, he sought the seat of the Attorney General in 1594 but he failed. One year later, he also failed to get the office of Solicitor-General. To ease the disappointment, Earl of Essex gave him an estate at Twickenham which he later sold.

In 1596, Bacon was appointed Queen's Counsel but this didn't help him get the office of Master of Rolls. Likewise, his financial situation was bad. At the same time, he fiancée Elizabeth Hatton broke off with him, allegedly for a wealthier man. He reached the low point in 1598 when he was arrested for debt. However, his prestige in the eyes of the Queen increased soon thereafter. He eventually became one of the learned counsels although this didn't help his financial situation. His prestige in the eyes of the Queen rose further when he broke off his friendship with Earl of Essex and took part in investigation against him for treason. He was also a part of the legal team in the case against Essex that resulted in the latter's execution.

Rise Under James I and Political Downfall

The accession of James I to the English throne marked a turning point in Bacon's political career. In 1603, he was knighted by the new King and four years later, he was appointed Solicitor-General. Meanwhile, he also married the young Alice Barnham, a daughter of an influential MP. He received a generous income which, however, wasn't generous enough for him to get out of debts.

After the King dismissed the parliament in 1610, Bacon managed to remain the King's favourite and retain good relationship with the Commons at the same time. In 1613, he finally got the long desired position of the Attorney General but his evident influence over James I arouse resentment among his peers. He continued to enjoy the King's affection and in 1617, he was appointed the temporary Regent of England and one year later, the Lord Chancellor. In 1618, he was awarded the title Baron Verulam and in 1621, Viscount St. Alban.

Despite being the King's favourite, Bacon's political career was over in 1621. Due to his debts, he was charged with corruption, sentenced to a fine of £40,000 and imprisoned in the Tower of London. The King helped him with both the fine and prison but he couldn't help him with his political career. He was declared incapable of holding office or seat in the Parliament and barely managed to avoid being stripped of his titles. Bacon devoted the last five years of life to studying and writing. He died childless in 1626.

Works

Bacon wrote on a variety of subjects that are generally divided into three categories:

    scientific works
    religious/literary works and
    judicial works

Some of his best known works include:

    The Great Instauration (Instauratio Magna)
    New Method (Novum Organum)
    Of Proficience and Advancement of Learning Divine and Human
    Valerius Terminus: on the Interpretation of Nature
    History of Life and Death
    New Atlantis
    The Wisdom of the Ancients
    Meditationes Sacrae
    Theological Tracts
    The Elements of the Common Laws of England
    Maxims of the Law
    Cases of Treason

Claude Levi-Strauss

Claude Levi-Strauss (1908-2009) is one of France's foremost thinkers of the 20th century. The celebrated philosopher and anthropologist is one of the key figures of structuralism and is along with Franz Boas and James George Frazer often referred to as the "father of modern anthropology" as he dramatically changed the Western perception of culture and civilisation.

Early Life

Levi-Strauss was born in Brussels, Belgium, in 1908. He grew up in France and was educated in Paris. After attending the Lycee Janson de Sailly and the Lycee Condorcet, he continued education at the Sorbonne in Paris where he studied philosophy and law. However, he soon gave up the latter and focused on philosophy. After graduating from philosophy in 1931, he taught at secondary school until 1935 when he took part of a French cultural mission to Brazil. At the Sao Paulo University, he became a visiting professor of sociology, while his wife Dina was a visiting professor of ethnology. Besides teaching sociology, Levi-Strauss also made several trips to the Amazon jungle where he lived and studied the native tribes.

Emigration to New York

After the outbreak of the Second World War, Levi-Strauss returned to France and took up arms. After France's capitulation in 1941, he left the country. He went to Martinique from where he emigrated to New York City. There, he taught at the New School for Social Research and at the Ecole Libre des Hautes Etudes which he co-founded with other French emigrates in New York including Henri Focillon, Jacques Maritain and Roman Jacobson. Levi-Strauss returned to Paris in 1948 to receive doctorate from the Sorbonne. One year later, he published his first notable work – The Elementary Structures of Kinship that soon became one of the most important works in anthropology.

Rise to Prominence

Although Levi-Strauss was well established among the academic circles by the mid-1950s, he rose to international prominence after he published Tristes Tropiques (A World on the Wane) in 1961. This partly philosophical and partly biographical account of his trips and life with the South American Indian tribes, and his next masterpiece – La Pensee Sauvage (The Savage Mind) that was published one year later laid the foundation for modern anthropology as well as Western understanding of culture and civilisation. In the later half of the 1960s, Levi-Strauss focused on a four-volume study, the Mythologiques which was finally published in 1971.

Honours

For his contribution to the 20th century thought and above all, anthropology, Levi-Strauss was honoured by many world's prestigious universities. In 1959, he became the chair of Social Anthropology at the College de France (he hold the post until 1982) and in 1973, he became a member of the Academie Francaise. He was also awarded honorary doctorate degrees from universities such as Harvard, Yale, Oxford and Columbia, memberships in academic institutions such as the National Academy of Sciences, the American Philosophical Society and many others. In 1973, Levi-Strauss also received the Erasmus Prize that is awarded by the Dutch Praemium Erasmianum Foundation for notable contributions to European culture, society or social science. Other Levi-Strauss' awards and honour include the Grand-croix de la Legion d'honneur, the Commandeur des Arts et des Lettres and the Meister-Eckhart-Prize, to mention only a few.

Later Life and Death

Levi-Strauss remained active after his retirement and continued to publish works on a variety of topics nearly until his death. He died in 2009, only a few weeks before his 101st birthday.

Main Ideas and Concepts

Claude Levi-Strauss is best known for his theory of culture and mind that revolutionised modern anthropology. He showed that culture is a system with underlying structures that are common to all societies regardless of their differences. Through his analyses he showed that patterns of structures including behaviour and thought are universal to all societies, and rejected the concept of primitive and modern mind, arguing that all men have the same intellectual potential. According to Levi-Strauss, all people think of the world around them in terms of binary opposites such as up and down, life and death, etc. and therefore every culture can be understood in these terms.

Levi-Strauss' ideas were heavily influenced by the so-called structural linguistics, especially the work of the Swiss linguist Ferdinand de Saussure (1857-1913). His works, however, also reveal the influence of Roman Jacobson and Franz Boas, both of whom he met in New York City. Other notable influences include Emile Durkheim (1858-1917) and Marcel Mauss (1872-1950).

Notable Works

Levi-Strauss published his first work Gracchus Babeuf et le communisme as early as 1926 but his most notable works were published only from the late 1940s to the early 1990s. The most important works by Claude Levi-Strauss include:

La Vie familiale et sociale des Indiens Nambikwara (1948)

Les Structures élémentaires de la parenté ("The Elementary Structures of Kinship"; 1949)

Tristes Tropiques ("A World on the Wane"; 1955)

Anthropologie structurale ("Structural Anthropology"; 1958)

Le Totemisme aujourdhui ("Totemism", 1962)

La Pensee sauvage ("The Savage Mind"; 1962)

Mythologiques I-IV (1964-1971)

Anthropologie structurale deux ("Structural Anthropology, Vol. II"; 1973)

La Voie des masques ("The Way of the Masks"; 1972)

Myth and Meaning (1978)

Paroles donnés ("Anthropology and Myth: Lectures, 1951-1982"; 1984)

Le Regard éloigné ("The View from Afar"; 1983)

La Potière jalouse ("The Jealous Potter"; 1985)

Histoire de Lynx ("The Story of Lynx"; 1991)

Plato

Plato (c. 428-427 BC ?€? 348-347 BC) is widely considered as one of the greatest thinkers of all times and is along his mentor Socrates and his student Aristotle regarded as one of the founders of Western science and philosophy. His thought is preserved in 26 dialogues which profoundly influenced the Western view of the world. Plato is also renowned as the founder of the Academy in Athens, the first higher education institution in the Western world.

Name Controversy

Diogenes Laertius, a biographer of ancient Greek philosophers reports that Plato's real name was Aristocles, just like his grandfather's. According to Laertius, the ancient Greek philosopher came to be known as Plato after his wrestling coach dubbed him Platon, allegedly for his robust figure as the Greek word "platon" translates into "broad". According to later sources, Plato's name is related to the broadness of his eloquence or the width across his forehead. Modern scholars, however, believe that the story about Plato's name is a legend, arguing that Plato was a very common name in his time.

Early Life

Plato's exact date and place of birth remain uncertain but he is thought to be born in Athens or the island of Aegina (17 miles south from Athens) sometime between 429 and 423. The celebrated ancient Greek philosopher was born into an influential aristocratic family. His father Ariston was according to the legend a descendant of Cordus, a semi-mythical king of Athens who ruled in the 11th century BC, while his mother was Perictione whose family was related to the renowned Athenian statesman, lawmaker and poet Solon. Plato's mother was also Charmides's sister and Critias's niece. Both were notable figures during the so-called Thirty Tyrants, a pro-Spartan oligarchic regime that rose to power after the Athenian defeat in the Peloponnesian War in 404 BC.

Plato grew up two brothers, Adeimantus and Glaucon, sister Potone and half-brother Antiphon. After the death of Plato's father, his mother married her uncle Pyrilampes whom she bore her fifth child. Plato's father is thought to have died while Plato was a child but the date of his death remains unknown.

Education

As a member of aristocracy, Plato was educated by the best teachers in Athens. He was initially a follower of Cratylus who introduced him to Heraclitean philosophy but he later became Socrates's pupil and declared himself as his devoted follower in the dialogue 'Apology of Socrates'. Relationship between Plato and Socrates isn't fully understood but in the 'Apology', Socrates mentions Plato as one of the youths he was accused to have corrupted, asking why their fathers and brothers didn't testify against him if the accusations were true. Later, Plato is also mentioned as one of Socrates's students who offered to pay a fine in behalf of their tutor to save him from death penalty.

Later Life

After Socrates's execution in 399 BC, Plato left Athens. He is thought to travel around Greece, Italy, Sicily, the ancient Greek colony of Cyrene (in present-day Libya) and Egypt. He returned to Athens in 387 BC at the age of 40 and founded the Academy, the first known higher education institution in the Western world. Plato's Academy operated until 84 BC when it was destroyed by Roman general and later dictator Lucius Cornelius Sulla. In the early 5th century AD, the Academy was reopened by the Neoplatonists but it was permanently closed by Byzantine Emperor Justinian I in 529. He saw it as a threat to Christianity despite the fact that the latter borrowed much from its founder's philosophy.

During his later life, Plato became involved in politics of the city of Syracuse in Sicily which was at the time a Greek colony. Diogenes Laertius reports that Plato first visited the city during the reign of the tyrant Dionysius the Elder (c. 432-367 BC) and impressed the tyrant's brother-in-law Dion who became his follower. The tyrant, however, eventually turned against the philosopher and sold him into slavery. He nearly died in Cyrene before he was bought freedom and sent home by an admirer. However, Plato was asked to return to Syracuse after Dionysius's death by Dion to become tutor to his nephew and the new king Dionysius II. The latter is thought to accept his teachings but the king distrusted Dion whom he had expelled from Syracuse. Plato was kept against his will by Dionysius II but he was eventually allowed to leave.

Death

Circumstances surrounding Plato's death remain uncertain. There are several accounts of his death, however, almost every account offers a different explanation. According to one account, he died in his bed while a young girl played on a flute, according to the second, he died on a celebration of a wedding and according to the third, he simply died in sleep.

Works and Influence

Although both life and works of Plato are surrounded by a number of legends and myths and despite the fact that many accounts are dubious, the influence of his thought on science and religion is perhaps greater than of any other individual. Directly or indirectly (mainly through Aristotle), Plato's view of the world dominated until the scientific revolution in the 17th century, while his arguments to prove that God exists and that human soul is immortal found their way into Christian theology.

Plato's works encompass 26 dialogues which are traditionally divided into early, middle and late period. Some of the most notable works of early period include:

    Apology of Socrates
    Crito
    Protagoras
    Meno

Of middle period dialogues, the most prominent are:

    Republic
    Symposium
    Phaedrus
    Phaedo

Most important late period dialogues include:

    Sophist
    Laws
    Statesman
    Critias
    Timaeus

Plato is also attributed 13 letters of which is best known the so-called Seventh Letter. However, authenticity of many is disputed which is also the case with some dialogues that are traditionally associated with Plato.

John Rawls

John Bordley Rawls (1921-2002) was one of the most influential American philosophers after the Second World War. He published his first book and widely considered his greatest work, A Theory of Justice, only in 1971 at the age of 50 but the book immediately came to be regarded as one of the most important works of political philosophy. His philosophy, also known as Rawlsianism received either strong support or strong opposition from political philosophers, especially the proponents of utilitarianism as Rawls's concepts challenge the utilitarian principles.

Early Life

John Rawls was born in 1921 in Baltimore, Maryland as the second son to one of Baltimore's most influential attorneys William Lee Rawls and his wife Anna Abell Stump Rawls. At a young age, Rawls and his family were struck by two tragedies. When he was 8 years old, Rawls got a contagious bacterial disease diphtheria. He recovered but his younger brother who contracted the disease from him didn't and died from complications. One year later, Rawls got ill from pneumonia. Another younger brother contracted the illness from him and died.

Rawls went to school in Baltimore and continued education at Kent School in Connecticut. After graduating from Kent School, he studied at the Princeton University. Soon after graduating from the Princeton University, Rawls was enlisted in the US Army and sent to the Pacific theatre, serving as an infantryman. The US Army offered him the position of an officer but he refused and left the Army.

Later Life and Death

After leaving the Army, Rawls returned to Princeton where he received a doctorate from philosophy in 1949. In the same year, he married Margaret Fox with whom he had four children. Until 1952, he taught at the Princeton University and then went to the Oxford University through the Fulbright Programme. Upon returning to the United States, Rawls began to work at the Cornell University as an assistant professor. In 1962, he became full professor at the Cornell University but in the same year, he took the position of a professor of philosophy at the Harvard University where he taught until the 1990s.

Despite his international fame, Rawls more or less lived a withdrawn life. Instead of becoming a public intellectual, he spent most of his time as an academic and family person. In 1995, he suffered a stroke which prevented him from continuing with his work. However, he was able to write three more books - The Law of Peoples, Lectures on the History of Moral Philosophy and Justice as Fairness: A Restatement which was published shortly before his death. John Rawls died in 2002, aged 81.

Rawlsianism

Rawlsianism describes the ideas and concepts of John Rawls but above all, the term describes Rawls's principles of justice as he presented them in his first and most influential book A Theory of Justice. In it, he introduced the so-called original position, a hypothetical situation involving hypothetical subjects who are given the task to create a political and economic system for a society in which they are to live after reaching an agreement. Each of the hypothetical subjects, however,

was put behind the so-called veil of ignorance which deprived them of knowledge about their social position, income, wealth, gender, religion, race and similar factors they could take advantage of to improve position for themselves and their immediate descendants. Rawls gave them only the basic knowledge about social organisation and human psychology, and knowledge of what he called social goods - things every rational person would want: opportunities, rights, liberties, wealth and self-respect. Rawls argued that his hypothetical subjects behind the veil of ignorance would agree on two principles of justice. They would agree that every member of the society should have 1) political liberty such as the freedom of speech, the right to assembly, the right to vote, etc. (equality principle) and that the social and economic inequalities are a) to the greatest benefit of the least advantaged and b) to guarantee equality of opportunity (difference principle).
Other Works and Concepts
Political Liberalism (1993)
Although his A Theory of Justice soon met criticism from many influential

philosophers of the time, Rawls didn't respond to his critics (except through his articles) until 1993 when he published his second book titled Political Liberalism. In the latter, he edited some of the concepts with which he dealt in A Theory of Justice but didn't depart from his main ideas. Besides responding to criticism of A Theory of Justice, Political Liberalism also deals with how to maintain just political system in the existing situations that are marked by philosophical, moral and religious diversity.

The Law of Peoples (1999)

In his third book, The Law of Peoples that was published in 1999 (first as an article in 1993) Rawls applied his theory of justice to international relations. Just like in A Theory of Justice, he developed his concept of how different peoples should interact and behave with one another on the basis of original position. He put representatives of different peoples behind the veil of ignorance with a task to develop principles that would govern international relations.

Lectures on the History of Moral Philosophy (2000)

This book is a collection of Rawls's lectures while he taught at the Harvard University.

Justice as Fairness: A Restatement (2001)

In the last book that was published before his death, Rawls responded to criticism of his most influential work but he also included an overview of his main concepts and issues he didn't address in his prior writings.

Two more books were published after his death in 2002:

Lectures on the History of Political Philosophy (2007)

A Brief Inquiry into the Meaning of Sin and Faith (2010)

Immanuel Kant

German philosopher Immanuel Kant (1724-1804) is considered the most influential thinker of the Enlightenment era and one of the greatest Western philosophers of all times. His works, especially those on epistemology (theory of knowledge), aesthetics and ethics had a profound influence on later philosophers, including contemporary ones.

Besides establishing himself as one of the foremost Western philosophers, Kant also made an important contribution to science and is considered one of the most important figures in the development of modern science despite the fact that he was most interested in philosophy of science and knowledge that science produces. His main contribution to the rise modern science was its liberation from theology.

Early Life

Immanuel Kant was born to Johann Georg Cant and his wife Anna Regina Cant as fourth of nine children. His (paternal) grandfather was from Scotland where the surname Cant is still relatively common in the north. Immanuel decided to change his surname from Cant into Kant in order for it to meet the German spelling and pronunciation practices.

Kant grew up under the influence of Pietism, a Protestant sect that was very popular in north Germany during the early 18th century. At the age of 8, he enrolled into a Latin Pietist school with an aim to study theology when older. However, he soon developed interest in Latin and the classics. At the age of 16, he entered the University of Königsberg and mainly dedicated himself to study of mathematics but he also began to develop interest in philosophy. In 1746, he was forced to leave the university due to his father's death. For nearly a decade, he worked as a private tutor for three influential families in order to help his younger siblings.

Later life and Death

In 1755, Kant returned to the University of Königsberg to continue his education. Within the same year, he received a doctorate from philosophy. He spent the next 15 years working as a lecturer and made a living from fees that were paid by the students attending his classes. But he also devoted a lot of his time to writing on various topics although his greatest masterpiece – the

Critique of Pure Reason was published only in 1781. A decade earlier, he finally became a professor at the University of Königsberg and taught metaphysics and logic until 1797. During the last years of his life, he became embittered due to loss of memory which severely affected his ability to work but he continued to write nearly until the very end of his life. He died in 1804, aged 80.

Personal Life

Kant was only 5 feet tall, thin and of fragile health. Nevertheless, he reached at the time extremely old age which he attributed to his strict daily routine. He got up at 5 o'clock every day and spent the next hour drinking tea, smoking his pipe and meditating. From 6 to 7 o'clock, he prepared for lectures he gave at home until 9 o'clock. He then worked in his study room until 1 o'clock and spent the next three hours dining, usually with his friends. After his only meal, he took a one hour walk and spent the afternoon and evening for reading and writing. The renowned German philosopher was completely dedicated to his work and never married.

Work and Philosophy

Kant's philosophy is often described as the golden middle between rationalism and empiricism. He didn't accept either of both views but he gave credit to both. While rationalists argue that knowledge is a product of reason, empiricists claim that all knowledge comes from experience. Kant rejected yet adopted both, arguing that experience is purely subjective if not first processed by pure reason. Using reason while excluding experience would according to Kant produce theoretical illusion.

German philosopher published his first work – Thoughts on the True Estimation of Living Forces in 1747. Explaining the nature of space, Kant rejected post-Leibniz rationalists, arguing that metaphysic methods can prove the existence of essential force. Afterwards, Kant mainly focused on philosophical issues although he continued to write on science and similarly as Leibnizian also criticised Newton's views.

First notable Kant's philosophical works were published only in the 1760s:

    The False Subtlety of of the Four Syllogistic Figures (1762)

Attempt to Introduce the Concept of Negative Magnitudes into Philosophy (1763)

The Only Possible Argument in Support of a Demonstration of the Existence of God (1763)

Observations on the Feeling of the Beautiful and Sublime (1764)

Inquiry Concerning the Distinctness of the Principles of Natural Theology and Morality, also known "the Prize Essay" (1764)

After taking the office of a professor at the University of Königsberg, Kant wrote inaugural dissertation – On the Form and Principles of the Sensible and Intelligible Work (1770), after which he didn't publish anything for more than one decade. But his next work, Critique of Pure Reason (1781) was followed by nearly a decade of original and influential works which turned the philosophical thought in a whole new direction. Kant's most influential mature works include:

Groundwork of the Metaphysics of Morals (1785)

Metaphysical Foundations of Natural Science (1786)

Critique of Practical Reason (1788)
Critique of Judgement (1790)

After the so-called critical period (named after his three Critiques, published between 1781 and 1790), Kant's health began to deteriorate rapidly but he continued to write. The most important works of the post-critical period include Religion within the Limits of Reason Alone (1793) and Metaphysics of Morals (1797).

Boethius

Boethius (c. 480-524/525) was one of the most influential early medieval philosophers. His most famous work, The Consolation of Philosophy, was most widely translated and reproduced secular work from the 8th century until the end of the Middle Ages. In the 9th century, Boethius's Consolation was also translated into Old English by King Alfred the Great (his authorship of the 9th century translation has recently been challenged) as well as later English by Geoffrey Chaucer, the author of The Canterbury Tales. Boethius is also credited with the spread of encyclopedic learning and transferring classical Greek knowledge to medieval Europe despite the fact that he didn't manage to translate all works by Aristotle and Plato as he intended due to his premature death.

Early Life

Little is known about Boethius's life before his imprisonment and execution in the 520s. He was born around 480 into an influential Roman aristocratic family of Anicii which produced two Roman Emperors –

Petronius Maximus (ruled 17 March – 31 May 455) and Olybrius (ruled April or May – October 23 or November 2, 472) as well as several Roman consuls. According to some authors, Pope Gregory the Great came from the Anicii family as well.

Most authors believe that Boethius's father was Manlius Boethius, Roman consul in 487 although many also think that his father may had been Boetios, the perfect of Alexandria c. 476. It is known that Boethius lost his father at a young age and was adopted by another influential aristocrat, Quintus Aurelius Memmius Symmachus who is thought to play an important role in Boethius's interest in philosophy and literature by introducing him to Greek-Latin learning and encouraging him to update it.

Where and by whom young Boethius was educated remains a matter of debate. The fact that he was fluent in Greek made many scholars believe that he may had been educated in Athens although many point out that a statement by Cassiodorus, a Roman statesman and Boethius's contemporary suggests that this wasn't the case. Many authors also suggest that young Boethius was educated by Ammonius in

Alexandria, especially those who think that his father may had been the perfect of Alexandria. Others, however, note that there is no evidence for him ever leaving the Italian peninsula.

Rise to Power and Downfall

Just like many of his ancestors, Boethius held important public offices in Rome. At the time of his birth, however, the Western Roman Empire no longer existed. In 476, the last Western Roman Emperor was deposed by a Germanic chieftain Odoacer who in turn was killed by Ostrogothic king Theodoric the Great. When Boethius was appointed consul in 510, the Italian peninsula was ruled by the Ostrogoths.

Thanks to his scholarly knowledge, Boethius's soon gained royal affection and in 522, he achieved appointment of his two sons, Boethius and Symmachus as joint consuls which he considered as his greatest achievement. In the same year, himself was appointed magister officiorum, the head of the government and court administration.

Boethius's political career seemed bright before he lost Theodoric's favour in 523. At the Royal Council meeting in Verona in the same year, he spoke in defence of former consul Caecina Decius Faustus Albinus who was accused of treason and conspiring with the Byzantine Emperor Justin I. Boethius's support to his colleague, however, didn't help either of the two because soon, Boethius was accused of the same crime. Three men stepped forward as witnesses and confirmed the accusations against Boethius. He was arrested and imprisoned in Pavia for one or two years before he was executed for treason. He was buried in San Pietro in Ciel d'Oro, an Augustinian church in Pavia.

Works and Influence

Boethius wrote his most influential work, the Consolation of Philosophy (Consolatio Philosophiae), in the year (or two years) before his execution. The Consolation which is traditionally viewed as the last great work of the Classical era had a major influence on medieval philosophy but it also profoundly influenced early Renaissance thought in Europe.

In the Consolation of Philosophy, written in a form of an imaginary dialogue with philosophy, Boethius argues that there is a higher power and that all the suffering has higher purpose. According to Boethius, the universe is ruled by divine love and true happiness can be achieved not through power and money but by turning to otherworldly virtues. This interpretation perfectly fitted with the Christian doctrine of humility and played an important role in the later Christian philosophy of consolation according to which suffering from evil will be rewarded in the afterlife.

Boethius's lifelong project – to translate all works by Aristotle and Plato - was never realised but he translated many works by Greek philosophers and helped transmit a significant part of the Greek knowledge to medieval Europe. Some of his most important translations include De Topicis Differentiis and De Arithmetica, while De Institutione Musica, a treatise on ancient music remained the most important work on Western music for nearly one millennium.

Seneca the Younger

Lucius Annaeus Seneca, better known as Seneca the Younger (4 BC – 65 AD) was a Roman philosopher, writer and statesman who is probably best known for being a tutor and advisor to emperor Nero. By the mid-1st century CE, he established himself as one of the most influential people of the Roman world but his influence turned out to contribute to his premature death. In year 65, Nero forced him to commit suicide for his alleged involvement in the Pisonian conspiracy to assassinate the emperor. Whether he was really conspiring against the last Roman emperor of the Julio-Claudian dynasty remains uncertain.
Early Life

Seneca was born into a wealthy and influential Roman family in 4 BC. He was born as the second child to Marcus Annaeus Seneca (also known as Seneca the Elder), a renowned and respected rhetorician and writer, and his wife Helvia. Just like his parents, Seneca's brothers also went into history. His older brother Gallio is known for meeting with St.

Paul in Achaea in the early 50s, while his younger brother Marcus Annaeus Mela was the father of the Roman poet Marcus Annaeus Lucanus, commonly known as Lucan.

Seneca was educated in the school of Sextii in Rome where he learned philosophy and received training for an orator. Due to poor health, his aunt took him to Egypt to live with her and her husband. He returned to Rome in 31 and according to his father's wishes, entered into politics. He was soon appointed quaestor but he also established himself as one of the most influential writers and orators in Rome as well as gained many influential friends including from the imperial family.

Exile in Corsica and Rise to Power

In 41, Seneca was exiled to the island of Corsica by emperor Claudius for his alleged adultery with the emperor's niece. During his exile in Corsica, he dedicated himself to writing and studying philosophy and natural sciences. Seneca was forced to stay in Corsica until 49, when the emperor's wife Julia Agrippina convinced Claudius to allow him to return to Rome. He was appointed praetor and tutor to the future emperor Nero. At the same time, he also built relationships with influential Romans including the prefect of the guard, Sextus Afranius Burrus.

Withdrawal from Public Life and Death

After Claudius' assassination in 54, Seneca and his friend Burrus became probably the most powerful and influential individuals in the Roman Empire. They were Nero's favourites but the new emperor's affection didn't come easy on them. In 59, they had to accept the assassination of emperor's mother Agrippina. After Burrus' death in 62, Seneca had enough of courtly intrigues. He decided to withdraw from public life and dedicate himself to writing but he couldn't escape politics. In 65, emperor Nero accused him of conspiring against his life and forced his former tutor and advisor into committing suicide. Most historians believe that Seneca probably wasn't involved in the Pisonian conspiracy.

Works and Legacy

Seneca created his best works in the last three years of his life although he was highly productive throughout his life. His most significant works include tragedies and philosophical dialogues but he was also interested in natural sciences. In 62, he wrote a scientific book titled Naturales quaestiones but other than discussing various theories, he didn't offer any original solutions.

The surviving works by Seneca include:

Tragedies (10 in total):

    Hercules Furens (The Madness of Hercules)
    Hercules Oetaeus (Hercules on Oeta)
    Phaedra
    Oedipus
    Agamemnon
    Thyestes
    Medea
    Troades (The Trojan Women)
    Phoenissae (The Phoenician Women)
    Octavia

According to most scholars, Octavia is highly unlikely to have been written by Seneca, while many also question some other Senecan tragedies, especially Hercules Oetaeus (Hercules on Oeta).

Dialogues (the most prominent ones):

Ad Marciam, De consolatione (To Marcia, On consolation)

Ad Helviam matrem, De consolatione (To Helvia, On consolation)

De Brevitate Vitae (On the shortness of life)

De Consolatione ad Polybium (To Polybius, On consolation)

De Providentia (On providence)

De Vita Beata (On the happy life)

Other prominent works by Seneca include:

Apocolocyntosis divi Claudii (satire; The Pumpkinification of the Divine Claudius)

De Beneficiis (On benefits)

De Clementia (On clemency)

Epistulae morales ad Lucilium (over 120 letters to Lucius Junior)

Naturales quaestiones

Cujus etiam ad Paulum apostolum leguntur epistolae (correspondence between Seneca and St. Paul; authenticity disputed by most modern scholars)

John Stuart Mill

John Stuart Mill whose writings on political and social theory, and political economy still hold significance is considered one of the most influential British philosophers of the 19th century. Initially a follower of Jeremy Bentham's utilitarianism, Mill later rejected all concepts that prevent the pursuit of spiritual growth and warned on the dangers of democracy as "tyranny of the majority".

Early Life

Mill didn't have an ordinary childhood. He was born in London in 1806 as the eldest child of Scottish historian, economist and philosopher James Mill who decided for a very rigorous approach to raising of his eldest son. Young Mill was kept away from children other than his siblings and was educated by his father. The latter who was a proponent of Bentham's utilitarianism wanted to create a genius who would continue Bentham's work.

We learn much about Mill's upbringing and education from his posthumously published autobiography. He writes that he was taught Greek when he was only 3 years old and to read works of Aesop, Xenophon and Herodotus by the age of 8 when he was also taught Latin and algebra, and introduced to Euclid's works. At the same time, his father made him the schoolmaster to his younger siblings. His education was focused on history and the works of Greek and Latin authors who were taught at the time. By the age of 10, Mill was reading Plato Demosthenes but his father also found it important for his son to study poetry. In spare time, young Mill was allowed to read novels and natural sciences.

Religion was excluded from Mill's education, however, at the age of 12, he was introduced to scholastic logic. One year later, his father introduced him to political economy through the works of Adam Smith and David Ricardo who was a close friend of John Stuart's father and often invited him to his home to discuss political economy. At the age of 14, he was sent to France to stay with a family of Samuel Bentham (brother of Jeremy Bentham). During the year he stayed in France, he attended classes at the Faculte des Sciences in

Montpellier where he was taught logic, chemistry and zoology but he was also introduced to many prominent French including Jean-Baptiste Say and Henry Saint-Simon.

Break with Bentham's Utilitarianism

At the age of 16, Mill refused to study at the Cambridge University or Oxford. Instead, he decided to work for a living as a clerk at the East India Company. One year later, he published his first article but he soon began to experience problems with his mental health. When he was 20 years old, he had a nervous breakdown which he attributed to rigorous study and lack of normal childhood. At the same time, he started questioning his views and became interested in art and poetry.

Changes in Mill's view became obvious in the articles he published in the 1830s, most notably "The Spirit of the Age" and "Civilization" as well as in his studies of Bentham (1838). He didn't break with the latter completely and recognised his contribution to philosophy but he rejected Bentham's concept of man and government, arguing that it doesn't give room for personal growth and ignores the dangers of democracy, respectively.

Later Life

In 1851, Mill married with Harriet Taylor whom he met two decades earlier. At the time he and Taylor met, the latter was married. Their relationship is generally described as deep friendship that didn't involve into a romantic relationship until Taylor's husband died in 1849. Taylor who was a women's right advocate and philosopher herself had a major influence on Mill and according to the philosopher, one of his most influential works – "On Liberty" which was published shortly after her death in 1858 was written jointly.

After his wife's death, Mill spent a lot of time in France at the house of his stepdaughter Helen Taylor near Avignon. In 1858, the British government assumed direct control of India and his function at the East India Company was abolished. He was offered a seat in a newly formed council of 15 members but he decided to retire instead. In 1865, he took the position of the Lord Rector at the University of St. Andrews and in the same year, he was also elected MP for City and Westminster.

During his brief political career, Mill advocated what he stood for including representation of women in politics, reform of the British government and changes in policy towards Ireland. His views were quite radical at the time and he wasn't re-elected at the 1868 general election. He retreated to Avignon where he died in 1873 from a bacterial streptococcus infection (erysipelas). He was buried next to his wife in France.

Works

Mill was highly productive throughout most of his life. He published his first article as young as 17 but his first major work – A System of Logic was published only in 1843. Other major works by Mill include:

Essays on "Bentham" (1838) and "Coleridge" (1840)
Essays on Some Unsettled Questions in Political Economy (1844)
Principles of Political Economy (1848)
On Liberty (1859)
Considerations on Representative Government (1861)
Utilitarianism (1863)

Examination of Sir William Hamilton's Philosophy (1865)
August Comte and Positivism (1865)
On The Subjection of Women (1869)
Autobiography (posthumously by Helen Taylor; 1873)

Heinz Duthel, Master in Philosophy
www.worldorganisation.net
www.organisationmondiale.com